ABC Animal Rhymes

By
Gaga

AKA Janice Abernethy
2nd Edition Interactive Videos

Copyrighted Material

Copyright © 2023 Janice Abernethy

Illustrations © 2023 Janice Abernethy

Website: jabernethy.com

Published by Professional Writers Help

Visit our Website: www.info@professionalwritershelp.com

E-mail: info@professionalwritershelp.com

ISBN: 978-1-962108-13-3 Paperback (6 x 9)

978-1-962108-14-0 Hardback (8 x 10)

979-8-9933573-5-5 Paperback (6 x 9)

Library of Congress Control Number: 1-12934600161

No portion of this book may be reproduced, stored in a retrieval system, or transmitted in any form or by any means, mechanical, electronic, photocopying, recording, or otherwise, without the written permission of the publisher.

Copyrighted Material

Dedicated to my
Grandson, Ike

Written and illustrated by:
Janice Abernethy, AKA GaGa
Clipart by: pnghut.com

A is for Armadillo

Armadillo, an animal that starts with an A,
Here is some information I would like to relay.

We live underground with the rabbits and mice,
We use our sharp claws to dig burrows real nice.

We're insectivores; We eat insects and bugs,
And our favorite meals are fat juicy slugs.

Don't touch me or eat me, cause you can get sick,
With leprosy, it's not a disease you might pick.

What else can I tell you? There is so much more.
But the butterfly is waiting. He's next on this tour.

B is for Butterfly

Butterfly, an insect that starts with a B,
I drink liquids from fruit and sap from a tree.

I pollinate plants and veggies and flowers,
By using my long tongue which has great powers.

My life has four stages, then I say goodbye.
Egg, caterpillar, chrysalis, and butterfly.

What else can I tell you? There is so much more.
But the camel is waiting. He's next on this tour.

C is for Camel

The camel, a mammal, begins with a C,
I live in the desert where nary a tree.

I have a hump on my back, some of us two,
Where I store lots of fat, believe me it's true!

I can use all that fat for water and food,
I can go days without water, isn't that shrewd?

What else can I tell you? There is so much more.
But the dolphin is waiting. He's next on this tour.

D is for Dolphin

I'm a mammal and dolphin which begins with D.
I like salty water, I live in the sea

Did you know that a killer whale isn't a whale?
A killer whale's the biggest dolphin you'll hail.

I have two stomachs and my food I don't chew
Although I am friendly, my enemy is you.

What else can I tell you? There is so much more.
But the elephant is waiting. He's next on this tour

E is for Elephant

Elephant, a mammal, which begins with E,
I can't jump, but I have a great memory.

When I'm in the sun I use mud for sunscreen,
I fill my trunk with water to get myself clean.

I am the largest land mammal as tall as the trees
But I'll tell you a little secret, I'm petrified of bees!

What else can I tell you? There is so much more.
But the fish is waiting. He's next on this tour.

F is for Fish

Fish starts with an F; I have a backbone,
They call me a vertebrate; that's how I am known.

Of main animal groups, fish are one of six.
Mammals, amphibians, and birds in the mix.

Reptiles, then invertebrates make up the rest,
But fish have gills and fins. I think we're the best.

What else can I tell you? There is so much more.
But the giraffe is waiting. He's next on this tour.

G is for Giraffe

A giraffe is a mammal that starts with G,
An herbivore who likes to eat leaves from a tree.

I weigh 200 pounds whenever I'm born,
And all over my body unique spots adorn.

I live in dry climates, savannas, grasslands,
No hyenas or lions, my only demands

What else can I tell you? There is so much more.
But the hippo is waiting. He's next on this tour.

H is for Hippopotamus

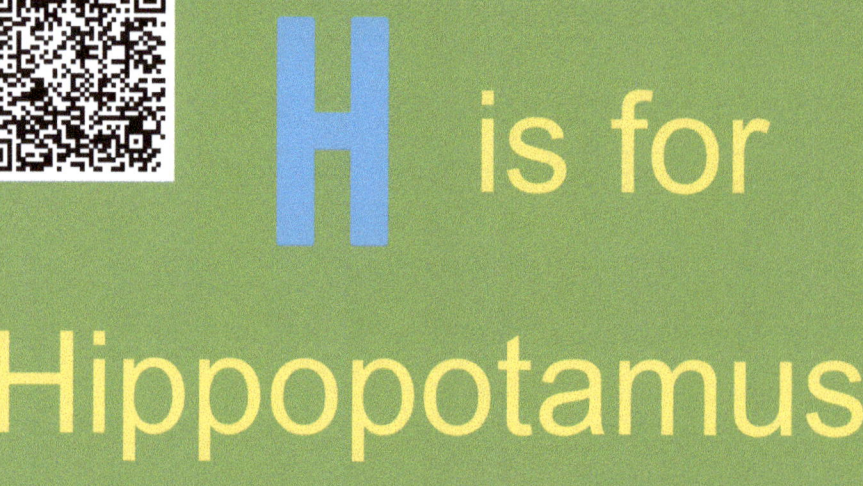

Hippopotamus starts with H, yes I know,
A mammal who is large that I call a hippo.

I sweat oily red liquid; I try to stay cool,
Spending my days in the water; hey I am no fool.

Hyenas, crocs, and lions are predators of mine,
But I am not frightened, I protect myself fine.

What else can I tell you? There is so much more.
But the Iguana is waiting. He's next on this tour.

I is for Iguana

Iguana, a reptile that starts with an I,
I'm a tropical lizard who lives way up high.

I'm a herbivore, my food is fruit, leaves, and flowers,
Keen vision and swimming, just some of my powers.

I have a long tail I can use as a whip,
Against predators like hawks, I just let it rip.

What else can I tell you? There is so much more.
But the jaguar is waiting. He's next on this tour.

J is for Jaguar

A Jaguar's a mammal that starts with a J,
Deer, fish, birds, and monkeys are just some of my prey.

I'm a carnivore which is why I like to eat meat,
I'm a cat that can swim; that is really quite neat!

In the jungle or desert is where I am found,
I can pounce on my prey with a leap and a bound.

What else can I tell you? There is so much more.
But the kangaroo's waiting. He's next on this tour.

K is for Kangaroo

Kangaroo is a mammal that starts with K,
And 200 pounds is about what I weigh,

Male 'roos are called bucks; Female 'roos are called does.
My predators are only wild dogs called dingoes.

A kangaroo's an herbivore, I don't eat meat,
I jump 25 feet with my really large feet.

What else can I tell you? There is so much more.
But the lion is waiting. He's next on this tour.

L is for Lion

Lion, king of the jungle, starts with an L,
And my roar is louder than you can yell.

Only boys have a majestic mane fit for a king,
But the girls are the hunters, isn't that something?

If you're close to a lion, keep an eye on your food,
If I am hungry I will steal it; I can be quite rude.

What else can I tell you? There is so much more.
But the monkey is waiting. He's next on this tour.

M is for Monkey

A monkey's a mammal that starts with an M,
An omnivore eats meat and plants with a stem

I'm really intelligent with a large brain,
Being so smart makes it hard not to be vain.

I belong to the primates, like humans and apes,
Living all over the world in all sizes and shapes.

What else can I tell you? There is so much more
But the numbat is waiting. He's next on this tour.

N is for Numbat

N starts the marsupial called a numbat,
I live in a log and I look like a rat.

I eat 20 thousand termites every day,
With my sticky tongue, they can't get away.

Main predators of mine can be snakes or cats,
Dingoes or foxes, birds of prey and all that.

What else can I tell you? There is so much more.
But the ostrich is waiting. He's next on this tour.

O is for Ostrich

An ostrich, a very large bird, starts with O,
I live wild in Africa, but not Mexico.

I'm the largest bird; I can grow nine feet tall,
My eyes are enormous; my brain's really small.

An omnivore I can eat both plants and meat,
I also like insects, they taste like a treat.

What else can I tell you? There is so much more.
But the pony is waiting. He's next on this tour.

P is for Pony

Pony, a hairy mammal that starts with P,
I am like a short horse, sometimes more feisty.

I am super strong even though I am small,
I eat grass in my pasture and hay in my stall.

Hanging on my neck is a beautiful mane,
I have a great memory and a big brain.

What else can I tell you? There is so much more.
But the quetzal is waiting. He's next on this tour.

Q is for Quetzel

Quetzal, a very striking bird, starts with Q.
Some think I'm the most beautiful bird, do you?

I eat small creatures like insects, bugs and more,
But I also eat fruit. I'm an omnivore.

Way up high is the Cloud forest habitat,
In Central America, that's where I'm at.

What else can I tell you? There is so much more.
But the Rabbit is waiting. He's next on this tour.

R is for Rabbit

Rabbit, a furry mammal that starts with R,
I'm a happy hare that can hop really far.

There is danger for me from a cat or dog,
I am prey to a bear, a bird or wild hog.

Some people think I'm cute and even like me,
But I eat their crops, they get angry, I flee.

What else can I tell you? There is so much more.
But the seahorse is waiting. He's next on this tour.

S is for Seahorse

Seahorse starts with S, an animal that's a fish
I live in the ocean and I'm rather smallish

I choose one mate and stay with them for life,
The husband carries the babies not the wife.

I may be the slowest swimmer in the sea,
Sometimes I use floating objects to help me.

What else can I tell you? There is so much more.
But the tortoise is waiting. He's next on this tour.

T is for Tortoise

A tortoise, a reptile that starts with a T,
Tortoises are turtles. I'm sure you agree.

Turtles have flipper legs and two back webbed feet,
I have elephantine legs and walk down the street.

I only like water for bathing and drinks,
And I am an herbivore, so I think meat stinks

What else can I tell you? There is so much more.
But the uakari is waiting. He's next on this tour.

U is for Uakari

Uakari is a mammal that starts with a U,
I live in the rainforest; this much is true.

My face is hairless; I'm a type of monkey,
I 'm an omnivore, my habitat is soggy.

I'm diurnal; I sleep at night, active at day.
My predators are humans, snakes, and birds of prey,

What else can I tell you? There is so much more.
But the vulture is waiting. He's next on this tour.

V is for Vulture

Vulture is a scavenger that starts with V,
I have a sharp hooked beak and talons on me.

My diet is animals decaying and dead
Body hunched, my neck is bare and so is my head

My beak is hooked and sharp, my wings are wide and strong,
But I do not have a voice box, so I cannot sing a song.

What else can I tell you? There is so much more.
But the walrus is waiting. He's next on this tour.

W is for Walrus

Walrus, a mammal that starts with W,
I live in the Arctic unless in the zoo.

Thick layers of blubber protect me from cold,
You know I can live up to 40 years old.

I sleep in the water; I have giant white tusks,
I eat worms, seals, crustaceans, and also molluscs .

What else can I tell you? There is so much more.
But the xerus is waiting. He's next on this tour.

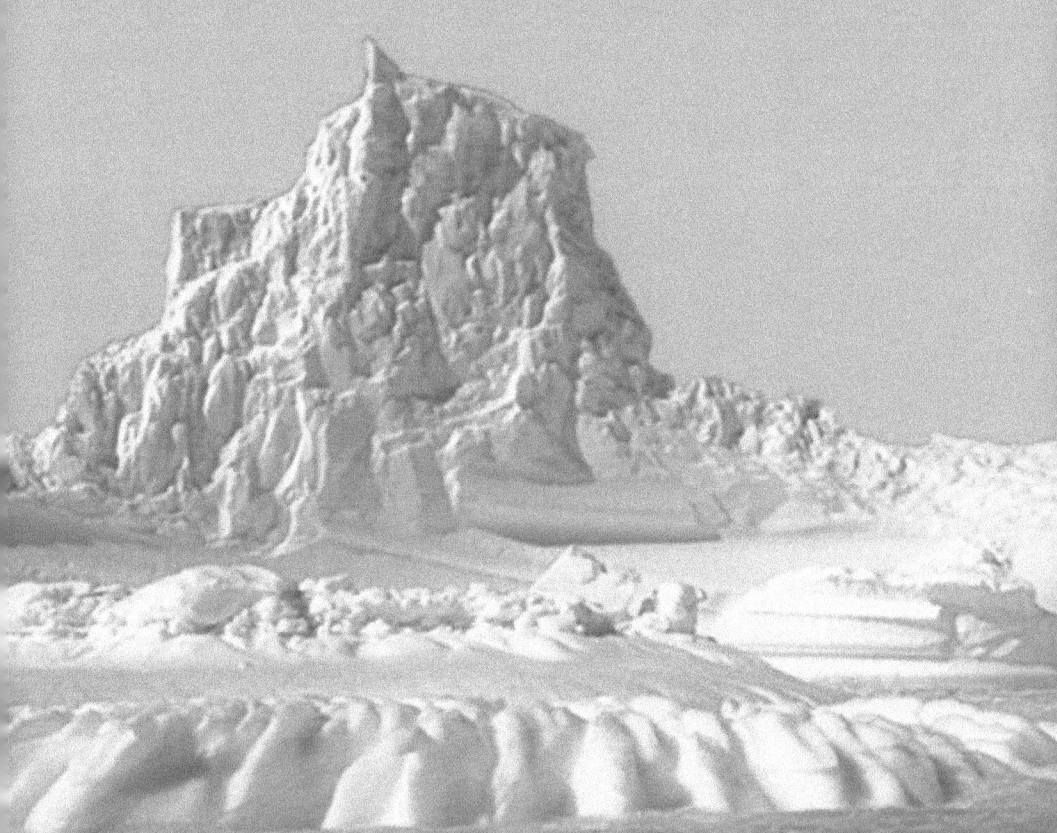

X is for Xerus

Xerus, a mammal that starts with an X,
My diet consists of nothing complex.

I eat insects, small animals, seeds and more,
I eat roots, eggs, and leaves. I'm an omnivore.

An African ground squirrel, I live in a burrow,
I am covered in fur from my head to my toe.

What else can I tell you? There is so much more.
But the yak is waiting. He is next on this tour.

Y is for Yak

A Yak is a mammal that starts with a Y,
I am one shaggy creature you cannot deny.

I am in Asia on the Tibetan Plateau,
Three miles above sea level, cold weather, you know?

I'm in the cow family; I'm an herbivore.
I eat grasses, mosses, and wild flowers galore.

What else can I tell you? There is so much more.
But the zebra is waiting. He's next on this tour.

Z is for Zebra

A zebra is a mammal that starts with a Z,
I'm an herbivore and in the horse family.

I'm covered with stripe patterns of black and white,
No two patterns the same, they're a unique sight.

Africa's my home where it's arid and dry,
I sleep standing up. Can you do that? Well try!

What else can I tell you? There is so much more.
But my dinner is waiting. There is no more tour.

About the Author

Janice Abernethy, known as Jan Ford, grew up in Mars, Pennsylvania, surrounded by her parents and five brothers. Her childhood was filled with playful interactions with her brothers, from playing school to engaging in sports like baseball. Jan's love for animals was evident, as she frequently brought home animals and dreamed of living on a ranch one day. She married her dream man, Sam, and together they had two daughters and a son. Despite her affinity for technology, she surprised everyone by pursuing a career in teaching. She worked tirelessly to obtain a degree in elementary and special education while caring for her family. Jan's teaching journey took her to Greenville Area School District, where she blended her passion for animals and nature with education. Her classroom featured various class pets, and she spearheaded a schoolyard habitat project with her students. After 23 fulfilling years in teaching, she retired alongside her husband, Sam. The couple enjoy their retirement on their farm, Abernethy Acres, filled with horses, and embark on RV travels across the country. Their grandson, Ike's birth inspired Jan to write a children's book, which she illustrated after teaching herself art through YouTube tutorials. The book, initially intended as a Christmas gift, was published to share joy with other children.

Jan's retirement projects, class websites, and blogs can be explored on her website, where she showcases her multifaceted talents. To learn more about the author or her teaching journey, visit her website at https://jabernethy.com.

www.ingramcontent.com/pod-product-compliance
Lightning Source LLC
Chambersburg PA
CBHW052034030426
42337CB00027B/5000